Thoughts and Feelings

Thoughts and Feelings.

Un   t ℝ

Thoughts

and

FEELINGS.

FARI QUÆ SENTIAT.   HORAT.

BY

ARTHUR BROOKE.

London:

PRINTED FOR LONGMAN, HURST, REES, ORME, AND BROWN,
PATERNOSTER-ROW.

1820.

Un   f ®

DEDICATION.

—◆—

YE gentle few, whose hearts, and lips, and
    eyes,
  With smiles, and kisses, and kind words
    have shed
A sweetness o'er the lonely paths I tread ;
Who know that in this outworn bosom lies
A soul yet quickening with some sympathies,
  Though the first fire of earlier days is fled,
  And the proud heart which long and vainly
    bled,
Submits no more to Love's indignities :—
Accept these lays: their sweeter, tenderer
    tone—
  If such there be—to you in sooth belongs ;
And well I hope—and in that hope alone
  This wreath I weave—that e'en some wilder
    songs
Which move the worldling's frown or cynic's
    sneer,
To you and some like you may still be dear.

Preface.

—

IN putting forth the present little Volume to the world, the Author is aware of the truth of the observation, that if a writer does not surpass himself at every successive publication, he is generally supposed to have failed, as, even if equally well written, there is no longer the stimulus of novelty for his style or opinions. This may more particularly be the case with regard to the following pages, which contain little or nothing of interest detached from their Author, but are mere transcripts of personal feelings and experience, which,—except in some splendid instances,—are apt to be considered, and not unreasonably, as insipid and uncalled-for obtrusions on public notice. Yet, however little calculated such effusions may be thought for the general reader, the Author could but feel gratified on former occasions, and encouraged on the present, by the spontaneous expressions of sympathy and approval which have reached him from quarters the most unexpected; and to those individuals he begs now to offer his acknowledgments:—he claims no merit but that of sincerity, and from a few congenial or indulgent spirits he has already received his reward;—to others he is indifferent.

Some points of objection which have been urged against his former productions may perhaps be anticipated for this: but as those objectors would be the least likely to understand his explanations or defence, the Author is content to pass them over in silence.

Canterbury, December, 1819.

CONTENTS.

APPENDIX.

1819.

P O E M S,

1819.

———◆———

SONNET.

═══════

Spirit of Song! whom sometimes I have wooed
   From thy close haunt by Castaly's dark well,
   If thou didst ever lend thy sacred shell
To cheer or soothe thy votary's solitude,
Accord it now! and be its strings imbued
   With all of Sorrow's sweetness, that the swell
   Of its deep notes may echo to the cell
Where the heart sinks in its most desolate mood.

There is a stony region in this breast,

Hard, hot, and barren, and the freshening spring

   Of Feeling, half-forgotten, sleeps below :

Yet are there moments when the Muse will bring

Her quickening wand, and at the touch confessed

   Sudden the emerging waters grateful flow.

A YOUNG GIRL'S ADDRESS TO HER MOTHER.

Nay, Mother, why that frown?
Is it a crime that I have found a way
To soothe a youthful poet's lonely hour,
One who has seen and suffered much, and now,
Shut out from all save three or two tried hearts
Which never fail him, dwells in Solitude?
Oh had you seen, as I have done, the glow
Of earlier years flush over his wan cheek

At my approach, and his most eloquent eyes,

Which had been talking with the sacred tomes

Of other tongues and ages, or with rapt

Unearthly glance followed his thoughts to heaven;---

Oh had you seen his cold and troubled look

(Where to the keen observer was confessed,

Through the forced calm of philosophic pride,

That pain, and fear, and doubt, and hope, and

      dread,

Were still the prisoned inmates of his heart)

When it met mine, whate'er its present mood,

Instantly change to such a cordial smile

As if his soul leaped forth to bid me welcome;---

Had you seen this, Mother, you could not chide me.

  Then would he talk of Knowledge, and the lights

Yet burning o'er the wreck of dim Antiquity,

Like meteors o'er a grave, by which he traced

The rise and fall of empires, and the ebb

And flow of intellect from clime to clime;

Though melancholy was the inference

He drew from his research; he said he wandered,

And so in his belief did other men,

Though they perceived it not, through the sad waste

Of life in error or uncertainty,

From birth to death without a hope or guide.

And of the inexplicable mystery

Which wraps our being, mournfully he spake.

Of Interest, Pride, and Prejudice, and of

The odious track in which men blindly plod,

And their fierce folly in defending wrong,

And of the dreams and lies which solemn fools

And wilier tyrants forge to lead along

The simple crowd, he told; and, somewhat
       moved,—

Of Faith, that many-headed monster, which

With blasphemous perversion has been fed

From age to age with human blood and tears!

And then he told me that the Law of Love

Alone should govern this uneasy world.—

Then as in eager converse oft we drew

Nearer together, he would gently bend

My form to his, and with a smile and sigh

Sink on my lips,—and oh! the subtile fire

Which from that touch shot through my thrilling
          veins!

Oh, Mother, you are old, you do not know,

Or have forgotten, haply never felt

The transports which two mingling spirits feel,

Who having long explored on painful wing

The unimaginable depths of Thought,

Find nothing to repose upon, but turn

And realize one blessing e'en on earth.

   At times in this tumultuous tenderness

My senses were o'erwhelmed, then would he seize

His harp, and bending o'er its silvery strings,

Call back my spirits, and compose his own.

Yes, it was thus when last we met, and these,

These were the strains he passionately sung.

Song First.

1.

Oh! love, in the depth of those melting caresses,

  In which our tranced spirits deliriously swim,

When I put back, all trembling, thy dark-flowing

    tresses,

  To gaze on those eyes so dissolving and dim;

When I feel in my arms all thy young beauties

    glowing,

  When round me that form clinging fondly I see,

I own, as I clasp thee with heart overflowing,

  That life yet hath left me one blessing in thee!

2.

Then damp not my joys by that sigh self-reproving;

   The Virtue *we* serve shall be Nature and Truth;

And the misjudging world may condemn us for loving,

   Who deem but of Love as the folly of Youth.

They know not that those in whose breasts it beats

     strongest,

   Have hearts to which wisdom its best lore hath given;

And that souls where its fervors divine have burned

     longest

   Are those best prepared for the raptures of Heaven!

Song Second.

1.

Sweet friend! if e'er the slumbering string

   Of this neglected lyre shall waken,

'Twill be when from the struggling wing

   Of Feeling custom's chains are shaken.

2.

When thou, in thy unfettered youth,
  Shalt stand triumphant by my side,
In love---in holiness---in truth---
  In all, save earthly forms, my bride.

3.

When free as light thy soul shall soar,
  Above the gross world's groveling throng,
And with extatic flight explore
  With me the heavenward source of song.

4.

Till proudly gazing from that height
  Where Wisdom's springs perennial flow,
We scorn the blind and envious spite
  Of the base crowd that crawls below!

5.

Robed in the intellectual blaze,
  Gathered at Truth's empyreal throne,
Like meteors o'er their blasted gaze
  On shall we pass---bright and alone!

6.

Or pausing in our high employ
  To taste a dearer, tenderer bliss,
What can our wishes frame of joy,
  That dwells not in our mingling kiss?

7.

And when our souls dissolving blend,
  And tranced in mutual raptures lie,
If earthly ties *must* have an end,
  Then, then, beloved one! we'll die.

SONNET.

THE sullen hue of this November sky
    Is dearer far to me than all the blaze
    Of summer suns, that with officious gaze
Seem to upbraid my unadmiring eye,
That wanders o'er creation heavily,
    Without the smiling glance of silent praise
    For all the verdant wonders which their rays
Work on the world with annual alchemy.

For this condensing atmosphere can lend
   Strength to the flagging spirits' wearied wing,
To soar in thought's high region, where we blend
   Our being with our minds' imagining,
And in the blessedness of that new birth
Mock at the meaner joys of this low earth.

SONNET.

THE following lines were composed under feelings of strong indignation on visiting the spot where a detestable and barbarous outrage had been recently committed by the Laws of England, on the body of a patriotic and unfortunate Spaniard. (See the daily Papers, Dec. 1818.*)

My foot falls heavy on the Hero's breast,
Who lies a cold and mangled corse beneath;
Unhonored and forgotten now the wreath
Which bloomed victorious round his patriot crest

---

* The following extract from one of them may not be unacceptable: " The shameful treatment of the Spanish officer who killed himself the other day, was, we grievously suspect, an intended compliment to the understood opinions of government on these subjects. This gentleman (Mariano Marquez de Castro) was concerned in the noble conspiracy of Porlier, that is to say, in a conspiracy to procure the very constitutional freedom which the vile Ferdinand had promised him in common with all his preservers. He was imprisoned in consequence, and subsequently got to England, where, instead of finding his patriotic countrymen taken by the hand by those who flattered and encouraged them to fight the French, he saw them struggling against poverty,

While battling for the Right.---Should he *thus* rest
   Whose gallant spirit nobly sought in death
   A refuge from disgrace, and whose free breath
Scorned the vile clay which Shame's dark bonds
       invest ?

Oh Thou that mockest at misfortune ! Thou
   That warrest with the dead ! Oh may the blight
Of lasting infamy upon thy brow,
   England ! for this all blisteringly light !
And when thou fall'st, as soon thou must, then be
Such mercy as thou shewedst, shewn to thee.

---

calumny, and hostility. It was a combination of these circumstances,
and the yearning after his unfortunate country, which drove him to put
an end to his existence."———" Crowds followed the body to the
burial place, and on its arriving at its destination, it was exposed
naked to the view of the public, who immediately expressed a feeling
of horror at the sight. After the body had lain in that condition for
a short time, *it was thrown headlong into the hole prepared to receive it. When it fell in, the noise caused a renewal of the expres-
sion of public indignation ! !*"

TO

———— ————.

Jane! if the glow of a moment could dart
Its warmth to the core of a passionless heart,
That hour which beheld our last wild-quivering kiss,
Had perhaps been more deeply remembered in this.

But no! through my breast though I felt the flame
        thrill,
That shrouded heart's pulse lay unwakened and chill;
As lightnings in vain pour their beams round a rock
Which secure in its coldness but smiles at the shock.

Ah! once beneath eyes of less luminous ray

My heart would have melted in softness away,

But when even *thy* glances have dwelt there in vain,

Oh! it never may hope those emotions again!

STANZAS.

How sweet to wanton with the trembling strings
   Of Woman's heart, and wake their tenderest tone;
Or sway with influence high the quivering springs
   Of tears which wait on thy commands alone!

And sweet when once the captive soul is freed
   Which pined whole ages in unpitied pain,
To make the breasts for which thou bleddest, bleed,
   And pay them trebly back those pangs again!

TO ———.

WITH SOME POETRY OF THE AUTHOR'S SET TO MUSIC.

If Music's breath can give a charm to words,
  Which feebly speak thy beauty's softening spell,
Oh! let some minstrel touch the impassioned chords.
  And tell for me what I may never tell.

Then haply one soft trembling drop may dim
  Those eyes, and in that breast one answering
    thrill
May wake a pardoning, pitying sigh for him
  Who loved—alas! perhaps who loves thee still!

SONNET.

TO AN ARTIST.

Painter! whose curious hand could fix the hues
  Of the soul's lineaments, and thus chain down
  On thy charmed tablet the unconscious frown,
Which pain and passion o'er the front diffuse,
Unlovely—though the meditative muse
  Perhaps not wholly may such look disown,
  But pitying spare from her own verdant crown
One sheltering leaf fresh with Castalian dews!—

Painter! perhaps thine art had here once found
    Far other exercise! in earlier years
Perhaps had traced a cheek all dimpling round
    With rosy smiles, an eye undimmed by tears
Or studious vigils, and the joyous glow
Which Thoughtlessness flings over Youth's bright
        brow.

TO

————— —————,

Oh Fanny! when thy fluttering pulse
   Is throbbing to my fiery kiss,
And passions, wild and high, convulse
   Our mutual frames, till o'er the abyss
   We hang of agony or bliss!
Tell me not *then* of holier ties
   Which round thy heart must ever twine,
Since all that's dear beneath the skies
   Friendship—Affection—Love—combine
   To make thee for that minute mine!

There is a claim I know—I feel—
 And mine must soon relinquished be,
Yet once more with my lip I seal
 My momentary right to thee,
  With rapture's unfeigned fervency!
And oh! when that embrace shall hold thee,
 In which alone thou darest to rest,
How close soe'er those arms enfold thee,
 Remember that thou once wert pressed
  As fondly to as fond a breast!

SONNET.

18th OCTOBER, 1817.

Seven years of Childhood's unconcern---seven years
  Of Youth's quick varying sense of joy and pain—
  Seven added years of Manhood's opening reign---
Have brought that heavy hour when hopes and fears
Grow cold, and when the fountain of our tears,
  Which once, like dew drops o'er the parching plain,
  Watered the heart, will never flow again,
Whate'er the weight the breast o'erburthened bears.

The future now avails not, since no time
  Can e'er unteach this knowledge—that we stray
Through life all helplessness, and blindly climb
  From Youth to Age, a dim and perilous way!
Which darklier ends (howe'er vain dreamers rave)
In one wide gulph, inscrutable,—the Grave.

C

STANZAS.

I CARE not when this scene shall close,
   No terrors hath the grave for me,
This wearied frame may there repose,
   And leave the encumbered spirit free:
   Or should it rot in apathy,
     And moulder with its mortal clay,---
     Oh God! 't were still a happy day
Which ends this fearful agony!

Hopeless on Earth, I turned to Heaven,
Till lost in Glory's boundless light,
All blind and blasted, downward driven.
I sunk in clouds of tenfold night;
And in the soul's perpetual blight
I drag about this hateful chain,—
But soon I shall not ask in vain
From thee, O Death, the wretched's right

SONNET.

Alas! we talk but to the winds, who speak
    Of suffering to the world's unthinking throng.
    They know not of what clay the child of song
Is fashioned, on whose frame such feelings wreak
Their torture, that the wildest words were weak
    To give them utterance ;—passions deep and
        strong,
    Pangs nameless, numberless, to him belong,
Though traced not always on his stoic cheek.

Ah fool! to think of sympathy from those
   Whose unimaginative eyes alone
Discern life's vulgar and immediate woes;
Love is too fond—Time will this truth disclose,---
   That while we dream there will be two or one
   Who feel with us---but wake---and there are none.

STANZAS.

1.

How small a deed of kindness, when the heart is
  sunk in woe,

Will sway the source of tears until their fountains
  overflow,

In breasts that in the bitterest hour of unrelieved
  distress

Had scorned to let one burning drop the pangs they

2.

Oh! well the soul can meet the shock of wrong,
    neglect, and pain,
Fenced in its icy panoply of undisguised disdain;
The storm may rave—that heart is firm, which soon
    before one ray
Of kindness from some gentle eye in softness melts
    away.

3.

A spirit that can wrestle with and overcome the rude
And angry tempests of the world, when in their
    wildest mood,
Can feel the touch of tenderness with deeper, surer,
    thrill
Than those who bend to every blast their weak and
    servile will.

4.

And oh! forgive, ye friendly few, if sometimes I
    have shewn

The semblance of a mind and heart, ah! too unlike
    your own;

Perhaps by woes you deemed not of my bosom then
    was wrung,

And scorpion-like my own sad heart each harsher
    accent stung.

TO

——— ———.

———

1.

Sweet Aura! when my spirits sink
 Beneath the clouds of care and pain,
'Tis yet some solace when I think
 How soon I meet thy smile again.

2.

Whate'er the woes which through the day
 Pursue me with unceasing blight,
Those griefs all melt in joy away,
 When in those arms I sink at night!

3.

And still my soul can almost be
 Content at morn and noon to grieve,
While it may spring, unchecked and free,
 To meet and mix with thine at eve.

4.

And dread not thou the envious sneer

   Of such as would our loves condemn,

Because they know, so pure, so dear

   A passion ne'er can throb for them.

5.

They have not felt---they ne'er shall feel

   That bliss when hearts commingling blend.

Which still the same through woe or weal,

   Love on unaltered to the end.

6.

For such must be the mutual tide

   In which our lives shall flow for ever,

Unless thyself the stream divide---

   And *can* that be?---oh, no. love, never!

TO

————   —— ———.

————————

1.

WHEN twilight dims the evening sky,

   And sparkling soft the stars appear,

To Halia's grove again I fly,

Where nightly I receive the sigh,

   And stay the trembling tear,

And calm the throb so deeply felt

When maidens first are taught to melt.

2.

Beautiful are the changing hues
    Which mark the sun's departing hour;
And lovely are the lucid dews
Which in the sleeping flowers infuse
    Their fresh and fragrant power;
But oh! more lovely, pure, and dear,
The virgin's blush---the virgin's tear!

3.

And think not, love, my vows untrue,---
    Although when many a maid before
Her feebler spells around me threw,
My vagrant heart escaping flew,
    And sought that maid no more;
Oh no! 'tis not for hearts like mine
Ever to fly from eyes like thine!

CONTRAST.

1.

THE hill was in brightness---the valley below
    Grew dim as the shadows of evening came o'er;
So my heart still reflected her eye's sunny glow,
    Though the cold clouds of sorrow hung dark at
        its core.

2.

And gaily the wild birds' sweet music ascended,
    Yet sadly the breeze sounded through the black
        pine;
As lately the laugh of her glad spirit blended
    Its innocent mirth with the murmurs of mine!

3.

As Nature's best beauties from contrast must borrow
    Their still-changing charm of harmonious delight,
So love, hate, and hope, fear, and grief. joy, and
        sorrow,
    In one sacred passion commingling unite!

TWILIGHT.

How sweet hath been this darkling pause!---
    But, lo, the emerging moon I see,
Whose envious light the veil withdraws
    Which screened awhile my love and me;
Beneath the shade we wandered free
    And mocked at man's obtrusive gaze,---
Then fair as Dian's orb may be,
    Love now might well excuse her rays!

Yon trembling star, whose radiance dim
   Burns faintly in the distant skies,
Is light, and light enough for him
   Who looks but in his lady's eyes;
The glow-worm's lamp a torch supplies
   To guide our steps through Halia's grove;---
Then why should worlds of brightness rise
   On those whose brighter world is Love!

STANZAS.

WRITTEN ON THE SEA SHORE.

1.

OLD Ocean is a sacred thing;
 Beneath the sun---beneath the moon---
Along this wild shore murmuring,
 It sings a ceaseless tune.

2.

I've seen on many a summer's eve
 The calmness of its azure plain
So smile, that thought could scarce believe
 'Twould ever frown again.

3.

I've watched on many a wintry night
  The maddening waves tumultuous roar,
As if their once-awakened might
  Would sleep in peace no more!

4.

Old Ocean! all thy moods are mine;
  But *I* beneath their changeful sway,
Sink to the grave in swift decline,---
  Thou,---smilest at decay!

SONNET.

WRITTEN UNDER A BEAUTIFUL DRAWING OF
JANE SHORE.

Ah gentle Shore! how oft I turn to gaze
    Upon thy mild and melancholy cheek,
    So softly tinctured with the last faint streak
Of Beauty's lingering bloom; while through the haze
Which sorrow sheds o'er the dim-burning blaze
    Of once-bright eyes, that smile, so sweetly weak,
    Fall- o'er thy faded lips, pale, pure, and meek,
Like evening flowers beneath a star's cold rays.

O fair and frail one! if thine earthly guise
   Were half so lovely as thy semblance here,
    And Man thy judge!---thou couldst have nought
       to fear
Of sufferings such as fablers old devise,---
   That sad sweet tale which won our infant ear,
Till we sat listening with down-streaming eyes.

SONNET.

TO A VERY YOUNG CHILD.

Young scion from a stock in which my blood
   Is no remotely blended! happy thou
   If ever on thy undistorted brow
This halcyon calm of Apathy could brood!
But when from its unconscious solitude
   Thy soul shall issue forth, the peaceful flow
   Of thy young days, as passions gathering grow.
May swell at last into the cataract flood
Of irremediable Woe!---But why,
   Ah gentle Boy, this augury of ill!
I envy not thy blessings: yet a sigh
   Steals from my breast while o'er thy slumbers
      bending.
To think my spirit may not be thus still
   When I, what thou art entering on, am ending.

SONNET.

ADDRESSED TO A SKELETON IN DR. ———'S STUDY.

Last night I saw---it may be in a dream---
　These withered bones stalk to my couch and say,
　With such unearthly tone that as I lay
Froze at my heart its life-sustaining stream;---
" Child of the dust! immersed in many a scheme
　Of fruitless care, know, thou hast but a day
　Ere co'd obstruction stops thy pulse's play,
And Death must quench thy being's vital beam!"

Speak yet again, thou griesly monitor,

 If an immortal spirit e'er possessed

This perishable frame, oh speak once more!

 Give but one sign---and I may guess the rest.

 Speak! move!---the dry bones mock my idle

  quest,

Shewing my soul but what it knew before.

France.

A SONNET.

Is not this land a happy one? which teems
  With all that eye could ask from side to side
  Of fair and fruitful, quickening far and wide
Beneath this genial sun's most living beams?---
Such *seems* her state---but is she what she seems?
  Or in her dark and torn heart does she hide,
  Writhing, the thunder-scars of blasted pride,
Watching the hour which Victory's wreath redeems

O Nature! why for that unresting thing

   Thy proud and fierce possessor, does thy womb

All-bounteous thus its ceaseless tributes bring,

While his rank breast by fell Ambition's sting

   Cankered decays, working his own sad doom,

   Folly his aim---his recompense a tomb!

SONNET.

WRITTEN IN A REMOTE VILLAGE ON THE CONTINENT.

Each one hath his own world: what are to me
 The dwellers in this rude and desolate place;
 Or I to them, who ne'er could know one trace
Of my existence,---joy or misery;---
Is each self-centered? or in his degree
 Is each to each essential, and the race
 Of man diffused over the world's vast space,
But one inseparable family?

I know not; but my heart hath proudly thought
    At times when maddened by the trampling throng,
That it could spare such fellowship, and sought
    How the deep woods and lonely vales among,
Its once not loveless nature might be taught
    To lose those feelings which it nursed too long!

TO ANNETTE ———.

Lausanne.

1.

SWEET Lausannoise! who wert to me
 A friend where other friends were not,
Whate'er thy future fate may be
 By one thou ne'er canst be forgot.
There is a heart that long retains
 The sense of kindness shewn like thine,
Which asked for all its gentle pains
 But one requiting smile of mine.

2.

I deemed this breast was steeled to pain---
   Yet could it not refuse a sigh
To think I ne'er should meet again
   The language of that loving eye.
May looks as kind and bright as those
   By thee to cheer a wanderer given,
Shed o'er thy pure life's peaceful close
   Their light, and guide thee hence to heaven!

SONNET.

To ————.

Lake of Geneva.

STILL present to the soul, though lost to sight!
  Sweet friend, I thought as through the vallies fair
  Of smiling France I roamed, wert Thou but there,
That prospect which around me bloomed so bright,
Would then be, oh! more dear—more exquisite;
  And its gay capital with thee would wear
  A happier aspect still, for thou couldst share
Joys which are lost upon a heart less light.

But oh! the loveliness—the power—of this
 Surpassing spectacle to feel with thee!
From blue waves which the soft winds scarcely kiss,
 To the far Alps in cloud-crowned majesty
To gaze, and gaze, till lost in the abyss
 Of thought we sank in rapturous sympathy!

ADIEU TO THE RHONE.

1.

ADIEU, adieu, thou glorious stream!

   Whose arrowy tide of azure glows

Beneath the sun's ascending beam,

   While in its pride it foams and flows!

Oh thus for ever may thy wave

   In life and joy and brightness shine,

And be thy spirit blest which gave

   Some portion of its health to mine.

2.

Too soon, alas! my joys are gone,

   Whilst thine can never know decay;

Still rolls thy strength increasing on,

   But mine must fail in one brief day!

In Freedom with the boundless sea

   To mix will be thy happy doom,

When this corrupted frame will be

   Consuming in a sunless tomb!

3.

Adieu! adieu! I ne'er may gaze,

   Swift Rhone, upon thy wave again;

Yet in the dream of after days

   'Twill flash across my mindful brain.

The lake that forms thy peaceful bed—

   The far-seen Alps—thy fertile shore

Which ne'er again my steps may tread,

   My visions may recall once more!

4.

Farewell, farewell, I linger yet,

Unwilling from these banks to fly;

E'en Albion's cliffs will now be met

By me with no rejoicing eye.

Who would not be an exile here,

Unshackled o'er such scenes to roam,

When not a thought or hope that's dear

Remains to tempt the wanderer home!

Paris.

—◆—

A SONNET.

Where the red stream of massacre once ran,
  Now giddy thousands crowd in thoughtless haste;
  Weak hearts and vain! unworthy of the waste
Of sympathy their fathers shared, when man
First raised his voice for freedom, and began
  That strife on which the world's high hopes were
      placed,
  That strife whose close its glorious birth disgraced.
And fixed on holiest cause the foulest ban!

And yet not wholly vain: that meteor bright

  Which should have grown into enduring day,

  Hath left a light which will not pass away:

Tyrants have seen and trembled at the might

Of banded brethren battling for the Right,

  And curse in silence their contracted sway.

TO AGLAE ——.

1.

WHERE'ER I roam! although the night
  Of care and pain hangs round me,
The beam that falls from looks of light
  Through every scene hath found me;
And though I know that splendid ray
  A meteor falsely guiding,
This heart will yet be lured astray,
  Though still deceived, confiding.

2.

When will my breast forget to feel
  Love's mingling pains and blisses?
And lips no more delight to steal
  This dangerous dew from kisses?
Oh, turn that ruby mouth from mine,
  Cling not to me so dearly,
Alas! thy soul can ill divine
  What mine feels so severely!

3.

Aglaë! yet an hour—and then
  Our lingering lips must sever;
And oh, my heart predicts that when
  We part, we part for ever.
I see o'er my devoted brow
  Fate's stormiest clouds collected,
But oh, as thus, be ever thou
  By Love's fond arms protected!

IMPROMPTU.

TO HARRIET AND MARY, WHILE TRAVELLING.

As tender flowers o'ercharged with rain
Bow their meek bells towards the plain,
So fair girls when spirits creep,
Their dissolving eyes to steep
In the balmy dews of sleep,
Droop their graceful heads, and fall
In sweet unconsciousness of all!

But let these eyes securely close
Their fringe in undisturbed repose,
For while they lie in slumber bound,
Love shall wake and watch around!

SONNET.

TO A STAR.

Fair Star! that rearest thy resplendent crest
　High o'er thy fellows, I have marked thy beam
　On many waters; thou didst softly gleam
Over Lake Leman's broad and peaceful breast,
And sweetly did thy pure reflection rest
　On the blue Rhone, and gay Lutetia's stream
　Joyed in thy light, and the great Sea did seem
Proud of the presence of its glittering guest.

'Thou on all these art shining now; and here
　As by the banks of Stour I lonely stray,
And meet once more upon its bosom clear,
　As I so oft have met, thy radiant ray,
I gaze—till all things round me disappear,
　And my soul flies o'er scenes far, far away!

FRAGMENT.

*   *   *   *

It is a blessed joy to float
   Upon the wings of our own mind,
Unpiloted to let our boat
   Drive carelessly before the wind:
To every gust of thought resigned—
   All effortless perhaps to reach
Knowledge which all the power combined
   Of studious lore could never teach.

Far o'er the future's misty track
   Now soaring with adventurous sail,
Or to the past now gliding back
   Rapidly with the changing gale:
Through many a scene of bliss and bale
   Like a pervading light to pass,
To turn from lifting Fate's dim veil
   To gaze in Memory's magic glass!

     *   *   *

        *   *

SONNET.

TO

———— ———,

Ah, friend! that is an unforgotten day,
  When wearied with long toil as we had been.
  Over Lake Leman's breast we sailed serene:
Stretched in our quiet boat we silent lay
From morn to noon, from noon till evening gray,
  So deeply gazing on that glorious scene
  That many a year must vainly intervene
Ere from our souls that sight can pass away.

Night came—but not as yet we sought the shore;
  We saw the stars come from the blue profound—
The distant Alps might be discerned no more—
  Dark Jura on the right the horizon bound
Cloudlike—the waves were slumbering, till the oar
  Awoke them gently with its measured sound.

SONNET.

THE whirl of wheels, the waftage of a sail,
   In swift progression over earth or sea
   May bear along this poor anatomy
Of wretched bones; but little can avail
The power of the hot steed or freshening gale
   To force the unwilling soul with them to flee,
   Which o'er the scenes it loves still wanders free,
And scorns the prison of this fleshly pale.

'Tis not because this dark and narrow room
   Closes around me, that I see no more
   Jura's proud height or Leman's peaceful shore:
No! the winged spirit can at will resume
Its pride of place, and with untiring plume
   Over that lovely land delighted soar!

TO MADELINA.

1.

AND we have met once more on earth,
　　And I have bade my spirit bow
Again before that might of Worth
　　Acknowledged long—developed now.—

2.

Not in proud Virtue's victory
　　To which e'en Fate subdued must fall,
But in that holier pride to be
　　For Virtue's sake subdued to all!

3.

I saw that pale and patient cheek,
  I saw—and 'twas some joy to see,—
That aspect settled, strong, but meek,
  Triumphant in humility!

4.

I saw a glory round thy brows,
  That halo, radiant, pure, and real,
Which Virtue sheds alone o'er those
  Whose steps have passed her stern ordeal.

5.

I heard thee as thy gathered breath
  In mild submissive accents broke,
I saw thee calmly bend beneath
  Thy yoke—not heavy—still a yoke.

6.

For thee too! who wert formed to soar
    Where vulgarer minds should sink or serve,
Whose once-unbending spirit bore
    All ills, but to submit or swerve!

7.

It should be well—the wise approve—
    And peace is in thy placid look;—
Yet should I not from thee remove
    Whate'er myself could never brook?

8.

Oh! why did not a light divine
    Illume my eager glance, when first
It met thee, and delivering shine
    Like that which o'er the Apostle burst?*

---

* Acts xii. 7.

9.

Before the warm dissolving touch
    Of Love should all thy fetters fall—
Yet, no, thou hast no need of such,
    To thee thy hope—thy Heaven, is all!

10.

I might have spared that fond embrace
    Whose cold return but seemed to say,
" Go ! seek some holier resting place
    Than on this erring breast of clay."

11.

I might have spared that rapturous kiss
    Which only drew a sigh from thee,
To think perhaps so mean a bliss
    Was all that seemed to wait on me.

12.

Forgive the poor attempt to wake
 Thy soul again to earthly love,
'Tis not for me—for man—to shake
 Affections fixed like thine above.

13.

My breast is any thing but pure,
 Though thine is of the pure the purest,
And I for thee must still endure
 Regrets which thou no more endurest!

AN ACTUAL DREAM.

This morn—'twas at the dawn of day,

A time when, as our sages say,

Visions are true—methought we lay

Under a shady myrtle bower,

Thinking of that quick coming hour

In which unconquerable fate

Dooms two fond hearts to separate.

Sadly we talked : and on thy lap

   Seemed to me then I saw unfurled,

(Almost I smile to think) the map

   Of this wide melancholy world :

And we with eager eyes would trace

   Each verge, to see if there were not

For us in all that mighty space,
  One little, bright, sequestered spot,
  Where we, with undivided lot,
Tranquilly might dwell and die,
Far from Man's malignity;
Who here would work us many a woe,
Because we from our souls would throw
Custom's cold and cramping chain:—
And long we searched —but searched in vain!
And then we turned in hopelessness
To take in one long wild caress
Our last farewell; one long, one last
Embrace;—Oh God! e'en that was past—
And thou wert gone!—This was too deep
A woe to bear even in sleep,
Sighs—sobs—from my full bosom broke,
And with hot stifling tears I woke!

f

MOONLIGHT.

1.

WHEN the busy world is sleeping,
  'Tis a joy divine to rove,
While the gentle moon is keeping
  Over-head a watch of love;
Just as if her lover lay
Underneath her guardian ray.

2.

All is hushed—so deep a calm
  Daylight hours can never know:
If there is in life a balm
  For the rankling breast of woe,
'Tis the lone and pensive bliss
Of wandering in a night like this.

3.

If the heart is tender still,
    Here are things enough to love,
The whispering bough—the sparkling rill—
    All Earth around and Heaven above;
Men are fearful things—but here
There are none to hate or fear.

4.

Here is not an envious eye,
    Here is not a slanderous tongue,
Here are none to mock the sigh
    Which their own unkindness wrung
From out a heart which would have died
Ere *they* should e'en in sport have sighed.

5.

Here if softness o'er us steals
    We may drop our tears at leisure,
Every thrill the bosom feels
    May indulge its own good measure;
Here our weakness none detects,
None derides, and none corrects.

6.

Better for him whose dream of bliss
    Morn's intrusive beam must sever,
If a night so sweet as this
    Which soothes him now, could last for ever;
Nor the bright sun rise again
To lead him to a world of care, and strife, and pain.

APPENDIX.

[It may be advisable to state that some of the annexed pieces were written prior to most of the published compositions of the Author what had been long missing had perhaps better have been lost, and at any rate it would have been easier to omit than to apologize for them, the reader must excuse their appearance as he can they may be interesting to the writer alone as records of his earlier feelings, which have not since undergone any material alteration, except, perhaps in their intensity.]

APPENDIX.

TO ———.

ON HER DEPARTURE FROM ———.

1816.

To think that Time may soothe my woes,
    And thy remembrance so decay,
Were bidding Life's dull business close,
    By tearing Hope's last charm away.

Yet still to love, but see thee blest,
    Perchance without one thought on me,
Or leaning on some worthless breast
    Which hardly deems what Love may be,

Must bring with it a keener thrill,
    And wrap me in a deeper gloom,
Than e'en that early sense of ill
    Which withered all my youthful bloom.

E 5

For long before this pang was known,
   My sickening heart had inward curled,
The spring, the zest of being flown,
   It turned disgusted from the world ;

To feel that love—the only thing
   Which life's delicious morn endears,
Conceals beneath the flowers a sting
   To poison all our future years :

To see the tide of time flow by,
   With all the cares and joys of men,
Yet meet with little worth a sigh,
   And nought to make me smile again,

Till that benign, endearing tone
   In which thy mild reproofs were dressed,
Those eyes that so consoling shone
   Shed comfort o'er my lonely breast.

I found that feeling was not dead,
   The clouds were clearing round my brow—
When oh! with thee the blessing fled,
   And all is worse than *tasteless* now !

TO ———.

1816.

1.

I SEE the shades of hopeless ill
O'er all the future thrown,
But it shall be my solace still
To bear that blight alone.

2.

The spell that on my bosom lies
Unseen, unshared, shall be,
And since to thee I cannot rise,
Thou shalt not sink to me!

The following Lines were occasioned by a midnight walk in the
country, after a conversation on that much disputed subject—
whether the note of the Nightingale is merry or sad.

1816.

1.

THE moon has sunk beneath yon hill—
    It is the midnight hour;
And in the dark horizon still
    The storms of evening lour.

2.

But there's a glowing, genial gale
    Breathes richly o'er the plain,
And sweetly in the distant vale
    Night's chantress pours her strain.

3.

Oh let none think her note is sad,
    For grief is *Man's* alone;
Earth—air—the whole creation's glad,—
    'Tis only lust to groan.

4.

The meaner brute a blessing found,
    To joys of sense confined,
On man the God of nature frowned,
    And cursed him with a mind.

AN EXCUSE.

1816.

ALL heedless of the chilling dews
　In yonder arbour laid,
We listened to the lyric Muse
　Till evening's deepest shade.

And who would not have lingered long
　In such delicious bowers,
To banquet on the breath of song
　Amid the bloom of flowers!

SONG OF A SPIRIT IN PARADISE.

1.

WE live in a round of fresh delights
　Still chasing each other away,
For Beauty and Love ever hallow our nights,
　And Wisdom ennobles our day.
Come hither, come hither, ye Children of Earth,
　And fly from that turbulent sphere,
All there you can fancy of bliss is not worth
　One moment of happiness here.

2.

Daily we quaff of the River of Life,
　Which must here to eternity flow,
And its waters are free from the anguish and strife
　Which embitter the draught below.
We feed on the fruit of that blissful Tree
　Which may not to man be given,
The taste is destruction to him, but we
　Ever feast on the Knowledge of Heaven.

TO MRS. ———.

Margate, 1816.

1.

AMID this gay unthinking throng
  One heavenly form I oft had seen,
Who moved with tranquil grace along,
  Serene and sweet as Beauty's queen.

2

A hope then in my bosom grew,
  Which reason now would vainly quell;
And feelings then my fond heart knew,
  Which now, alas! 'twere vain to tell.

3.

For I have marked how fond and free
  A *husband's* twining arm hath bound her,
These eyes have seen distractedly
  The pledges of his love play round her!

4.

Silence must o'er my passion close,
  She may not hear—she dare not heed:—
My lonely heart must hide its woes,
  Unknown must break—unpitied bleed.

IMPROMPTU REPLY,

TO A LADY WHO WISHED THE AUTHOR JOY ON HIS
BIRTH-DAY.

For the *joy* that you wished me I can't but allow
　　My thanks to your kindness are due,
But I'd rather, my love, you would *give* it me now
　　Than *wish* it me all the year through!

The following, almost extemporary, translation, was written at the request of a Lady who wished to have some idea given her of the Greek Ode prefixed by Moore, to the first volume of his Anacreon.

LAUGHING, quaffing, singing,
　Elegantly gay,
Roses round him springing—
　The Teian Minstrel lay ;
And all the little loves were there,
　Sporting some in airy dances,
While some the fatal shafts prepare
　That wound the soul through Beauty's glances ;
And some from those delicious bowers
Gathered the choicest sweetest flowers,
And while a fragrant crown they wove,
Proclaimed Anacreon, King of Love !
Wisdom from the azure skies
Bending down her awful eyes,
Through a smile she scarce could hide
Thus began the bard to chide ;—

" Why, Anacreon, vainly gay,
Why thus trifle life away,
Thou whom the wise are wont to call
The first and wisest of them all ?
Ever in light luxurious measures
Singing of Love's unhallowed pleasures,
Or drowning in Lyæus' bowl
The thinking spark—the immortal soul.
Why, old man, thus vainly gay,
Why thus trifle life away ?"
Mildly the graceful bard replied ;—
" Cease, O Goddess, cease to chide !
Although with thee I have not dwelt,
Nor at thy shrines in reverence knelt,
Yet me the wise are wont to call
The first and wisest of them all ;
Seizing each moment as it flies
'Midst balmy lips and beaming eyes ;
O'er nectared cups I wake the strain
Which tells of Love's delicious pain ;
For ah ! my lyre's inglorious tone
Can speak, can breathe of love alone !
Thus through the peaceful vales of life,
Far from the haunts of care and strife,
'Tis thus I laugh my days away,
And what is wiser—Goddess, say !"

TO —— ——.

ON HER UNJUST SUSPICIONS.

NAY, think not I would e'er estrange
    Thy lover from that constant breast,
I would not tempt the dove to range
    One moment from its hallowed nest.
Oh! if 'twere given to me to rest
    Within such pure devoted arms,
I feel I might e'en yet be blest,
    Though life has lost all other charms!

TO ———.

ON HER REQUESTING ME TO WRITE A POEM TO HER.

Nay, set me not this tuneful task ;
    Alas! to woo the vagrant Muse,
Is all that Jane of me could ask
    That I could e'er to Jane refuse.
For ah! my lyre at love's decay
    Sunk slumbering scarce to wake again ;—
Then if for once I disobey,
    Forgive me, Jane, forgive me, Jane!

STANZAS.

My harp was as that airy shell
  Beneath the breeze's fitful play,
Whose tones with every tempest swell,
  And with each dying gale decay ;
Now murmuring sorrow's softer sighs,
Now echoing loud its agonies.

Those sounds are hushed : despair has taught
  My soul its fruitless plaint to cease,
Silent to bear the strife of thought,
  But feel that patience is not peace ;
My heart and harp their last have spoken—
The strings of both, at once were broken !

VERSES

ON SEEING THE ANCIENT SYMBOL OF INDEPENDENCE,—
LA COCARDE BLEUE, IN CANTERBURY—JUNE, 1816.

Those who recollect the state of political feeling in this city about the time alluded to, will be at no loss to account for the sensations which produced the following lines.

1.

Oh Thou! that caught'st thine azure dye
From the pure tincture of the sky!
In Freedom's sight thou dearer gem
Than the proud despot's diadem!

2.

There *was* a time thou shon'st from far
In Virtue's cause the Polar Star;
There *was* a time when iced by thee
Men dared to grasp at Liberty!

3.

None know thee now : ah ! where are they
Who hailed thee in thy better day ?—
Some in the cold grave mouldering lie,
And some live on in infamy.

4.

Bright stranger ! if thou canst not brook
On fallen, faithless, hearts to look,
From these degraded mansions fly,
And mingle with thy native sky !

INSANIRE JUVAT.

To-night, to-night we twine, boys,
    A chain of the brightest hours;
Then bring, then bring me wine, boys,
    And scatter these rosy flowers!
Not often hath such a madness
    My bounding bosom thrilled,
But to-night must the cup of gladness
    Up to the brim be filled!

Then away with Truth and Reason—
    To-night let Love and Mirth
Make for a bright brief season
    A Heaven on this dull Earth!
We think not of to-morrow,
    But be it storm or shine,
'Twill take whole showers of sorrow
    To cool this tide of wine!

Then bring, then bring me wine, boys,
    And scatter these rosy flowers,
For to-night, to-night we'll twine, boys,
    A chain of the brightest hours!

CANTERBURY RACES.

A Fragment.

~~~~~

" That sarcastic levity of tongue
The stinging of a heart the world hath stung."

r

The following fragment,—the fruit of an idle half hour or two, would not have been reprinted (being entirely of local and temporary interest) but in conformity with the practice hitherto invariably adhered to by its Author, of publicly acknowledging any thing in the shape of personality which may have proceeded from his pen At the same time he takes the opportunity of deprecating the charge of having any share in those vulgar and violent productions with which the said city has of late been so plentifully supplied.

.

CANTERBURY RACES.

1819.

———

Canto First.

———

I.

HOW sweet, to pull one's night-cap o'er one's ears,
 And put on slippers " easy as old shoes,"
And with a pen, which neither cares nor fears,
 Set about courting (as they say) the muse,
Mixing a mass of truths with gibes and jeers,
 Which some will love, some laugh at, some abuse ;
Careless of critics, scribble—blame—praise—banter ;
Which bards call riding Pegasus a canter !

II.

And this I'll try for once, although, Heaven knows,
   Not often is my heart in such a mood:
Not often can it burst that cloud of woes
   Which shrouds it in its misty solitude.
Though even when the soul most joyous shews
   'Tis not because no bitter thoughts intrude,
But a wild mockery of pangs within,
Like Agony's involuntary grin.

III.

I'll play the fool in freedom here, for well
   I know that those I write to, oh! the pity,
That my unwilling Muse the truth must tell—
   They'll never understand me if I'm witty!
Even Aldermen disdain to read or spell,
   (As scandal whispers through this cursed city)
Though last week I was told—I just remember,
One means to learn by *the 14th of September.*

IV.

But I hate politics—no Tory I—
  Bawling for King and Church—the Throne—the
     Altar;
No place-pursuing Whig, whose envious eye
  Watches the hour when Ministers 'gin falter;—
I hold no bond with Hunt's rebellious fry,
  Who if they don't deserve, half tempt a halter;—
I never drained for Lushington one tub,
Nor spouted at the Independent Club!

V.

Of these enough; yet could I ever find
  That Party sprung from principle, that men
Would bear no longer to be led like blind
  Besotted asses by the nose,—then, then
Perhaps e'en *I* should not be found behind
  In any cause in which the sword or pen
Had power to right the oppressed, or aid the free,
To trample in the dust damned tyranny!

VI.

But these are themes too serious—let me see—
This is the WEEK, in which our annual Races
Are celebrated—though, what's that to me,
Who never shew my face at such gay places ;
Black-legs on Barham Downs I never see,
Because not there belike, and if the Graces
Dance in Saint Margaret's Street, I never know it,
Or, Heaven defend!—perhaps I should turn poet.

VII.

Lo! what a precious flock of fools and knaves,
Where pleasure blows her penny-trump, comes
             trooping,
Old dowagers with one foot in their graves,
And pale-faced pensive maids for husbands drooping ;
There ballad singers bawling stupid staves,
There bumpkin farmers hallooing and whooping ;
There Cyprian damsels screaming—God knows why—
As if *their* time for screaming wasn't gone by !

VIII.

But in this motley throng I'm sure to see
   Subjects to furnish out a pretty satire;
And that be sure is joyful news to me,
   Whose muse hath long been mum for lack of matter.
I cannot tell—perhaps she'll make too free—
   I only warn you she's not given to flatter.
And so God help you, Priests, 'Squires, Maidens all,
Pell-mell upon you in my next she'll fall!

IX.

There's not a Dean whom Ale-drinkers revere;
   No Savage watching fierce his fowls and fish;
No blockhead Baronet—no pompous Peer,
   No Military Miller, should she wish
To hold up for her sport she'd fly or fear,
   But lay them forth like lobsters in a dish;
And if they struggle, fix her fangs the faster in,
Regardless of what scrapes she gets her master in!

Canto Twelfth.

I.

Canto the twelfth! by all the Gods I'm tired!
   I think you must confess I've had a job;
My Pegasus I thought would have expired
   Before he'd half got through this well-dressed mob.
The Muse, although for the occasion hired,
   Quite out of breath begins to pant and sob,
And with a hearty curse on all, determine
No more to waste her verse upon such vermin.

II.

The thing's not to my taste, I must confess,
  But when we once have taken up our pen,
And thoughts and images upon us press,
  We scarce know how to lay it down again:
This " ancient city" seemed too in distress
  For want of one whose intellectual ken
Could pierce through character, and let folks see
All are not just that which they ought to be.

III.

In the description of the *Fancy Ball*
  Of Wednesday evening last, I think we shone ;—
A pleasant sort of thing enough, where all
  Take " *characters*"—who have none of their own.
But those who joy in song satirical
  May turn to my tenth canto, where is shewn
How up-g own babies met to play the fool—
I wonder they weren't whipped and sent to school

IV.

A few I then forgot, I'll mention now :—
  There stood a youth, whose recreant bosom wore
Ribbons of blue and buff; his sunken brow
  Intemperance stamped ; his hand a cudgel bore ;
He seemed t' have just escaped a recent row,
  With muddy plasters thickly spattered o'er ;
A pretty *Fancy dress* this !—by the blood
Of his Great-Uncle ! is *this* * * * ?

V.

No, no, *he* would be found when Freedom fights
  Against combining factions, at her side,
Combatting nobly for her children's rights,
  Not with her worst and meanest foes allied ;—
But *is* it thus his budding fame he blights ;
  Is this his independence—this his pride ;
The puppet of a party—the poor tool
Of a place-hunting gang ?—" Oh fool, fool, fool !"

VI.

With lowering look then came an ex M. P.
    Who having caught an ugly trick of leaving
Old friends for new, was forced too late to see
    His fol'y by his fall ; there's no retrieving
A lost good name ;—yet soured as he may be,
    I don't perceive he's fallen away by grieving.
Ten times my Muse had half a mind to prick him,
But hang it! when a man's down we won't kick him.

VII.

So let him pass, disguised as Solomon :
    He's at " *St. Stephen's*" still, and I don't see
For my part where's the difference when all's done—
    Save at his farm he has better company.
And since he yields in eloquence to none,
    Whene'er he would exert that faculty,
Instead of stupid Tories and vile Whigs,
He may harangue his ploughmen or his pigs.

VIII.

Not much here of the ladies; they'll excuse
  Th' omission, probably the less the better;
I know no *good* of them, and though the Muse
  Would twenty times have lashed them, had I let her,
I thought 't would be ungrateful to abuse
  Those pretty play-things, in whose flowery fetter
Although I sigh no longer, yet at times
They serve to fill up leisure hours or rhymes.

IX.

And now adieu, my slender gray-goose quill!
  Though to the very stump thou'rt worn away,
Let folly and my foes remember still
  We have another, which no distant day
May tempt on them to exercise its skill;—
  And for my very courteous readers, they
Just as they choose may like or leave these lays—
I dread no censure, and expect no praise.

THE END.

Ingram Content Group UK Ltd.
Milton Keynes UK
UKHW020653240323
419106UK00007B/586